THE BEST OF

MATT

1991

MATTHEW PRITCHETT studied at St
Martin's School of Art in London and first saw
himself published in the *New Statesman* during
one of its rare lapses from high seriousness. His
cartoons have also appeared in *Punch* and the
Spectator, among many other publications.
He has been *The Daily Telegraph*'s front-page
pocket cartoonist since 1988.

The Daily Telegraph

THE BEST OF

1991

'I'm not doing the test for
seven-year-olds – I'm at the
Primary School of Life'

CHAPMANS

Chapmans Publishers Ltd
141-143 Drury Lane
London WC2 5TB

First published by Chapmans 1991

© The Daily Telegraph plc 1991

ISBN 1–85592–589–3

A CIP catalogue record for this book is available from
the British Library

Photoset in Linotron Times and Optima by
Monoset Typesetters, London
Printed and bound in Great Britain by
Cox & Wyman Ltd, Reading

THE BEST OF

1991

'What happened to the Silly Season?'

'It's the new Government health warning – I come with the packet'

It's a Funny Old World

'It's the recession'

'I see the Martians still haven't got round to mowing your lawn'

'So it's settled then, we give up the mobile phone and have a baby instead'

'I wasted all that time reading this novel and it didn't even win the Booker Prize'

It's a Funny Old World

'It's a sad story – he used to be Nigel Kennedy's tailor'

'Oh dear, my dahlias have opted-out of the Chelsea Flower Show'

'He's captured brilliantly
the lack of facilities,
transport and cheap
housing in rural areas'

It's a Funny Old World

'Look, he's coming out of the closet'

'I suppose that's another one of those jobs you'll never get round to doing'

'Type yourself a letter of
apology for what I did at
the office party last night'

'Storm winds could mean a
dangerous build up of
Christmas aftershave in
eastern areas'

It's a Funny Old World

'Due to heavy demand, I can only allocate you 10 per cent of the presents you've applied for'

'I'd just like to thank all you wonderful people – if it wasn't for you I'd be at home watching the Oscars on TV'

'Look, there's that nice
couple we met here last
bank holiday'

'Guinness has been
good for us'

'So, tell me about your life as a social worker in Orkney'

'It doesn't necessarily mean
his wife is trying to kill him'

'Oh dear, I can't remember
if I locked my back door'

Crime

'And it was absolutely nothing to do with the West Midlands Serious Crime Squad'

BR Regrets . . .

'Sorry I'm late. My train arrived on time, I fainted and missed it'

'Darling, your season ticket has arrived'

'Did you have a good day at
the railway station, dear?'

'Apparently the British
have 37 different words
for BR'

Essex Man

'Oh dear – I suppose I've lost my no-claims bonus now'

'I can't understand it, Kenneth Baker is usually so gentle. He's never done anything like this before'

'I've finally found a dog
that compensates for my
own inadequacies'

'If you turn me in, I'll
tell them you never paid
your poll tax'

The Chunnel

'No, sorry mate, this isn't
the French Eurotunnel
team speaking'

'I don't think this counts as
swimming the Channel, sir'

'I can hear a government
subsidy but I don't
think it's coming this way'

'I did it bowing to
Prince Charles'

'We're popping into town this afternoon, would Princess Anne like a lift?'

A Westerly Airstream . . .

'We've reason to believe you've been using a hose-pipe on this beanstalk, Jack'

'Then I got out of the hose-pipe business and moved into selling sun-ray lamps'

'Keep scraping – it's the
weather forecast in
a minute'

'I think we're safe now,
the worst of the claims
seem to have missed us'

Church Times

'Do you come to these enthronements often?'

'Sorry, you're not hip enough'

'I suppose you'll be free to go shopping on Sundays now you're retiring, Dr Runcie'

'Arthur's gone to buy a DIY greenhouse and I've come to pray it doesn't fall down'

'We Are Gone'

'I didn't want Mrs Thatcher to see me wearing a grey suit'

'. . . And if anyone rings, promise them my support'

'There's a 10p fine every time you say "It's the end of an era".'

'Well, it's part of the enterprise culture, isn't it?'

'We Are Gone'

'Of course, Mrs Thatcher
may pop back and check up
on the decor now and again'

'Look out, I think he's
got Mrs Thatcher's speech
in there'

'Have you noticed that prime ministers are looking younger these days?'

'We're forces loyal to John Major and we've come to secure his victory'

That Tax

'Specialist subject: local
government finance,
March 18-21, 1991'

'If a poll tax form has your
name on it, there's nothing
you can do about it'

'I haven't got the heart to send Mrs Thatcher her poll tax rebate'

'Well, that's the Complete Works of Shakespeare, now let's think of an alternative to the poll tax'

That Tax

'Blenkinsop, go and knock down the east wing, please'

'I doubt if we'll see
European monetary union
in our lifetime'

'I'm doing a road pricing
experiment for the
Government – 50p please'

Politics

'She has the look of someone who knows where the NUM funds are'

'I won't kiss you if you're just going to give me a lecture on proportional representation'

'We've spotted a Liberal Democrat – they're extremely rare'

Politics

'They're Roderick's
contribution to the new
classless society'

'I didn't sleep a wink. I'm so
excited about the
Citizen's Charter'

'Give it to me straight,
doctor, just how much of
a political issue am I?'

'One's been given the
Government's NHS plans
and the other's got
Labour's alternative'

Health

'Could you make me just a bit better for £2?'

'I'm drinking to forget that someone else invented it first'

'Only when there's an aaargh in the month'

'I've run out of newspaper –
I'll wrap them in a
Government healthy diet
report instead'

'It looks as if the England fans
have been here as well'

'Typical, you arrive at
prison only to find the
Germans have got
there first'

'Paul Gascoigne's gone. I sold
him to an Italian police
station for £4 million'

'Would you rather watch
the rain at Wimbledon or
the rain at Lords?'

Sport

'Well, that's the first
setback for the
England team'

'The England cricket team
are coming in . . . They'll
probably be out again in a
few minutes?'

'You didn't let him
watch the McEnroe
match, did you?'

'I couldn't get any
strawberries so I got you
sauerkraut instead'

Trade Wars

'What do you think, could
I pass it off as
a French poodle?'

'We've had reports that your sheep are worrying French farmers'

'Waiter, this fly in my soup – it isn't French is it?'

The Phoney War

'This is one of your less good ideas, Saddam'

'I'm just going the extra mile for peace'

'I suddenly fancied a
holiday'

'We're thinking of
deploying you 87.3 metres
from the Kuwait border,
Mr Backley'

Pump Wars

'And don't tell people you work for a petrol company – pretend you're a poll tax collector'

'That's what they say when they find out the price'

'I can't remember the exact
date of birth, but I know
petrol was £2.27'

'We traded in the Fiesta –
this needs no petrol and
hardly any water'

Pump Wars

'Well, OF COURSE nobody understands you!'

'Can you siphon off the
expensive stuff and put in
three gallons of the
cheaper stuff?'

Baghdad Blues

'I must go, darling, my wife thinks I've been rescued from Baghdad by Ted Heath'

'Prepare to be boarded!'

'You were right – he's not going for a khaki election'

Desert Storm

'I'm sure it's not breaching
security to tell me if you
take milk and sugar'

'I just went along to the
Boat Show and they
packed me off to the Gulf'

'Gentlemen, this shows one
of our snowballs hitting
a girl from form 3c'

'The Day of All Mothers
is about to begin'

Desert Storm

'Just as I suspected, more
Iraqis trying to break in'

'A delicious contribution
to the war effort from the
Belgians, eh Sarge?'

*'Mr Major came all this
way and you had to ask him
about the hard Ecu'*

Desert Storm

'The war's not over until
Sylvester Stallone feels safe
enough to fly to Europe'

'I think we've stumbled on an Iraqi arms dump'

'I keep being kissed by jubilant British soldiers who've heard about the interest rate cut'

Cleaning Up

'We've been called to clean-up the Gulf'

'I'm worried about the environment – does it look like leaded or unleaded?'

'We've got every shade of
green from Dark Seaweed
to very pale Environment
White Paper'

Options for Change

'Would you sponsor
my battalion?'

'It's a rat race, you take the test at seven, and you're burned out by eight'

'Iraq is massing troops on the Saudi border, inflation is heading for 10 per cent, there are record mortgage arrears and you are worrying about a few paltry A-level results'

Recessional

'Frankly, I'm just glad
to have a job'

'It's the recession
– I'm going to have to let
Bashful and Sneezy go'

'Why don't we lower interest rates and just not tell Robin Leigh-Pemberton?'

'I've bn mde rdndnt'

Recessional

'This is a hold-up. Move slowly towards the till and buy something'

'This used to be a really nice Jobcentre until the middle classes moved in'

'. . . and on that farm he had an overdraft, ee-i-ee-i-oh'

'Excuse me, madam, you've given me a jittery pound'

Recessional

'. . . and this is the ghost
of your Access bill yet
to come'

'And at 70 mph all you
can hear is the sobbing
of the workforce'

'I hope you'll ring off
before the charges go up
in September'

'I'm afraid there's
a 43.5p charge for
my phone number'

High Flyers

'I've given myself an
enormous pay rise but I put
an X for no publicity'

'We want an improved pay
offer and an extra "bong" at
the beginning of each
programme'

'And why can't you get a pay
rise that would cause
a public outcry?'

Foreign Affairs

'Raisa Gorbachev just can't
put down that biography of
Nancy Reagan'

'Do you mean in the
twelve months it has
taken me to tunnel
from East Berlin . . . ?'

'I get these palpitations
every time I think about
Dan Quayle'

London Zoo

'And if you want me to roar,
it's an extra £5'

'I hate these stupid
sponsorship deals'

'Maybe I could get a prowl-
on part in one of David
Attenborough's films'

'It's a jungle out there'